The Library of
Political Assassinations

The Assassination of
John F. Kennedy

Lauren Spencer

The Rosen Publishing Group, Inc.
New York

To history teachers everywhere, and to DJ Eldon, whose help and support were invaluable.

Published in 2002 by The Rosen Publishing Group, Inc.
29 East 21st Street, New York, NY 10010

Library of Congress Cataloging-in-Publication Data

Spencer, Lauren.
The assassination of John F. Kennedy / by Lauren Spencer.
p. cm. — (The library of political assassinations)
Includes bibliographical references and index.
Summary: Examines the political events leading up to the assassination of President Kennedy, the shooting itself, and its effects on American society.
ISBN 0-8239-3541-8 (alk. paper)
1. Kennedy, John F. (John Fitzgerald), 1917–1963—Assassination—Juvenile literature. [1. Kennedy, John F. (John Fitzgerald), 1917–1963—Assassination.] I. Title. II. Series.
E842.9 .S66 2002
364.15'24'092—dc21

                                              2001003324

(Previous page) President John F. Kennedy, who was assassinated on November 22, 1963.

Contents

Senator Edward Kennedy stands before the eternal flame that marks the grave of his brother President John F. Kennedy.

Introduction

The assassination of John Fitzgerald Kennedy, the thirty-fifth president of the United States, is perhaps one of the most analyzed events in American history. Mystery and controversy continue to surround his assassination. For some, that gruesome moment in Dallas, Texas, on November 22, 1963, marked the end of a national innocence and the beginning of the political and social upheaval often associated with the 1960s.

When President John F. Kennedy (commonly referred to as JFK) took office, he was not only America's youngest president, at the age of forty-two, but he was also the first Catholic elected to the office. By the time he made that fateful trip to Dallas, Texas, he had served for three years. Although his presidency was cut short, Kennedy left a rich personal and political legacy.

At the time, though, not everyone was enthusiastic about the Democratic president's activities in office. Kennedy scheduled this trip to Texas a year before his planned run for reelection. He hoped that the trip would bolster relations between his administration and the powerful, largely Republican, conservatives of Dallas. During the 1960 presidential election, residents of Dallas had overwhelmingly supported Kennedy's Republican opponent, Richard M. Nixon. It looked as though many city residents would support Republican Barry Goldwater in the upcoming 1964 presidential election. Although JFK was fully aware of the antagonism many Dallas residents felt towards him, he also believed in the power of reaching out and connecting with both the people and the politicians of the city.

No one could have predicted that his visit would turn deadly. The assassination of President Kennedy forever altered the manner in which the chief executive of our nation interacts with, and is protected from, the people around him. Kennedy was shot as he sat in a convertible automobile with the top down. Never again would a U.S. president sit in a vehicle without the protection of a bulletproof shield.

When Kennedy was shot on that November afternoon, presidential assassination was not a federal crime. As a result, the Dallas police force led the investigation into Kennedy's murder. It soon became clear that the magnitude of such a crime would require the use of federal agents such as those working for the Federal Bureau of Investigation (FBI) and the Central Intelligence Agency (CIA).

The assassination also marked major cultural and technological shifts in the United States. Television news came of age covering both the assassination and its aftermath. Networks also televised the arrest and the subsequent murder of the lead suspect in the Kennedy shooting, Lee Harvey Oswald. Rarely had the nation witnessed such real-life drama on television.

Perhaps the most enduring legacy of the Kennedy assassination is not concrete. For many Americans the assassination resulted in a crisis of faith, challenging their belief in the mythic America that Kennedy had come to represent. In 1963, half of the country's population was under the age of twenty-five and had come of age in an economically thriving America.

Kennedy came to represent the youthful vigor and optimism that seemed to infect many Americans. He was young, rich, and powerful. He spoke convincingly of his dedication to freedom and equality. Supporters considered him the idyllic family man, with a loving wife and two young children.

In a 1961 poll conducted by *U.S. News & World Report*, 70 percent of Americans stated that they trusted their federal government. Thirty years later, in 1993, that figure had dropped. A poll by the same journal revealed that only 29 percent of Americans believed that the government would do the right thing for its people. Clearly, many events during those three decades served to alter people's faith in government, but for many the assassination of John F. Kennedy came to represent the beginning of a very complicated, and at times dark, period in American history.

A Dark
Day in Dallas

On Friday, November 22, 1963, *Air Force One* touched down at Love Field, Dallas, Texas, at 11:40 AM. It was a sunny day, and as the president and First Lady Jacqueline (Jackie) Kennedy deplaned they were met by thousands of people hoping to catch a glimpse of the couple. Jackie Kennedy, who rarely accompanied her husband on political trips, looked nervous but smiled and waved in what would become her trademark pink Chanel suit. JFK walked directly up to the crowd at the airfield fence and began shaking hands with people before getting into a convertible limousine and heading into the city.

Dallas in 1963 was a wealthy city in northern Texas with more than 600,000 residents. Many residents were not terribly fond of Kennedy's policies. The morning of the president's arrival, a full-page advertisement sponsored by the American Fact-Finding Committee in the *Dallas Morning News* accused President Kennedy of being soft on Communism and listed several of his foreign-policy decisions as evidence.

The Motorcade

After leaving the airfield, Kennedy's motorcade drove into the city, along with Texas governor John Connally and his wife, Nellie Connally. Consisting of several vehicles, the presidential motorcade would be traveling through Dealey Plaza, greeting Dallas citizens as it made its way down Houston Street. There, the motorcade would turn onto Elm Street, past the Texas School Book Depository (a clearing-house for the state's textbooks), and onto Stemmons Freeway. Ultimately, the caravan would stop for a luncheon at Dallas's Trade Mart. Many of the city's police officers were on hand to keep order among the thousands of spectators lining the route in Dealey Plaza's park.

President Kennedy and Jackie Kennedy arrive at Love Field with Governor John Connally on November 22, 1963.

The first car in the procession carried Secret Service agents and Dallas's police chief, Jesse Curry. Next came the president's big, blue Lincoln convertible. Governor

This picture was taken as JFK's motorcade rolled through Dallas. It is one of the last images taken of the thirty-fifth president while he was still alive. Governor Connally and his wife, Nellie, are riding in front.

Connally and Nellie Connally sat in the front seat and JFK and Jackie sat in the back. On both sides of the car rode twin police motorcycle escorts. Behind them, a car filled with more Secret Service agents followed. Agents sat inside the car and some stood on the car's running boards, scanning the crowd. Vice President Lyndon Baines Johnson, his wife, Lady Bird Johnson, and Texas senator Ralph Yarborough followed in another convertible. Bringing up the rear were more Secret Service cars, the mayor's car, and buses carrying journalists and government officials.

The Fatal Moment

Many Dallas residents came out to see the president and wave at the passing motorcade. Spectators standing on the grassy knoll, or small hill, in front of the book depository had a perfect view of the president waving and smiling as his car slowly turned onto Elm Street. Suddenly a loud crack interrupted the parade-like scene as President Kennedy clutched his neck and turned toward Jackie. She cried out, "Oh my God, they have shot my husband!"

Jackie supports her mortally wounded husband as his motorcade speeds through the streets of Dallas on the way to Parkland Memorial Hospital.

Governor Connally was shot and collapsed onto his wife in the limousine. Another shot hit Kennedy in the head, jerking his body violently onto his wife's lap. Seconds later, Jackie climbed out onto the back of the limousine, as Secret Service agent Clint Hill climbed up on the trunk towards her. The car picked up speed with Hill still clinging to the trunk. The limousine raced to Parkland Memorial Hospital, Dallas's leading trauma center. The time was 12:30 PM.

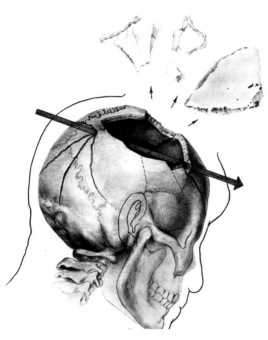

This drawing depicts the path of the bullet as it traveled through President Kennedy's head and exploded, destroying his skull.

Parkland Memorial Hospital

The president arrived at Parkland Memorial Hospital at 12:36 PM. Doctors could still feel his pulse and rushed him into surgery. Despite all efforts to save him, John F. Kennedy died.

At 1:00 PM, United Press International (UPI) news service announced that President John F. Kennedy had died from massive head wounds. Jackie had never left his side. Even as doctors attempted to save his life, she remained in the room, putting her wedding ring on his finger as they pronounced him dead. Doctors operated on Governor Connally, hoping to repair the extensive injuries he sustained to his back, chest, wrist, and thigh. After several hours in surgery, hospital doctors announced that he would make a full recovery.

A New President

In the meantime, Vice President Johnson waited at the hospital and debated his next step. Fearing that he too was in danger, Secret Service agents returned Johnson to *Air Force One* at Dallas's Love Field. There, Johnson could communicate with the White House staff. At that time, half of the presidential cabinet was en route to a conference in Japan. When they heard the news of the assassination, they returned to Washington, D.C., and awaited instruction.

The Secret Service wanted Johnson to return to Washington, D.C., immediately, but he refused to leave without Mrs. Kennedy, and she refused to leave without her husband's body. Finally, Kennedy's coffin was loaded onto *Air Force One*. At 2:38 PM, just two hours after John F. Kennedy was shot, Johnson took the oath of office at the back of the airplane to become the thirty-sixth acting president of the United States.

Vice President Lyndon Baines Johnson hurriedly takes the
oath of office aboard *Air Force One* with President
Kennedy's widow, Jackie, at his side.

Within the hour, nine out of ten Americans knew about the shooting in Dallas. The sixty reporters who had been traveling with the presidential motorcade sprang into action when they realized what had unfolded. Newspapers had already gone to press for the day, so radio and television became the main sources of breaking news. Television news anchor Walter Cronkite reported the assassination from CBS (Columbia Broadcasting System) studios in New York, making CBS the first television network to officially report the event.

Tracking Down a Suspect

As President Kennedy was being rushed to Parkland Memorial Hospital, Marrion Baker, one of the motorcycle police officers who had accompanied the presidential procession, dismounted his motorcycle and ran into the Texas School Book Depository on Elm Street. The building faced the motorcade route. At the time of the shooting, Baker reportedly saw pigeons flying off the roof of the depository. This led him to believe that the shots had come from the direction of the depository. Several other witnesses also reported hearing gunfire in the area around the depository.

Baker found the building's superintendent, Roy Truly, and together they began searching the premises. They found Lee Harvey Oswald, an employee at the

A shield of boxes forming a sniper's nest is arranged on the sixth floor of the Texas School Book Depository in Dallas.

depository, standing and drinking a soda in the cafeteria on the second floor. He was not detained. A little later, at a 1:00 PM roll call of depository employees, Oswald had seemingly disappeared. As a search of the building continued, Deputy Sheriff Luke Mooney discovered three empty bullet cartridges and several boxes arranged in what appeared to be a sniper's nest on the sixth floor.

Near the sixth floor exit staircase, police also found a bolt-action Mannlicher-Carcano rifle among some boxes. While a search of the depository was in full swing, Dallas police received a radio call from a citizen reporting the fatal shooting of police officer J.D. Tippit only a few blocks away. The description of Tippit's assailant matched the description of the man witnesses claimed to have seen in the depository window. Lee Harvey Oswald matched both descriptions.

Police went to the scene of Tippit's murder. Eyewitness reports from people who recognized Oswald from radio broadcast descriptions of JFK's killer led them to the Texas Theater a short distance away. There, Oswald sat watching the movie *War Is Hell*. Inside the theater, the police apprehended Oswald, a twenty-four-year-old, slender man of medium height with black hair, wearing a white jacket, white shirt, and dark trousers. Although he put up a struggle initially, the police subdued their suspect and arrested him. As the police took Oswald into custody, television news cameras filmed Oswald, who was loudly proclaiming his innocence.

President Kennedy

Born in 1917 to Joseph and Rose Kennedy, John was the second of nine children. His great-grandfather, Patrick Kennedy, was a farmer from Ireland who came to the United States in the mid-1800s and settled in Boston, Massachusetts. Jack (as he was often called) was born with an unstable back and a weak adrenal gland that left him open to infections. This ailment, later diagnosed as Addison's disease, kept Jack bedridden during much of his youth.

After graduating from high school, Jack attended Harvard University. He then joined the U.S. Navy, serving as a navy commander during World War II. In 1943, he became a war hero, having rescued fellow crew members of the Patrol Torpedo boat #109 after the vessel was rammed by a Japanese destroyer.

Interestingly, as a young man, JFK was not particularly interested in politics, but after his older brother Joe Jr. was killed in World War II, Jack's father began grooming him for the presidency. After returning to Boston in 1946, Jack ran for a seat in the House of Representatives and won. During his campaign, he often invoked the slogan "The New Generation Offers a Leader." In 1951, he was elected to the Senate.

Then-senator John F. Kennedy and his bride, Jacqueline Lee Bouvier, cut the cake after their wedding at St. Mary's Church in Newport, Rhode Island, on September 12, 1953.

Marriage and Family

It was during his time as senator that Kennedy met Jacqueline Bouvier, a beautiful socialite who came from a family of Catholic aristocrats of French descent. She worked for the *Times-Herald*, a local Washington, D.C., newspaper and met JFK during an interview. They were well matched and made a dazzling couple. In 1953, John and Jackie married and had a family that included Caroline and John Jr. (known as John-John). Tragically, Jackie had given birth to a girl, who was stillborn, and a young son, Patrick, who died from respiratory failure when he was only a few days old. His death came just three months before the presidential visit to Dallas.

Profiles in Courage

JFK won a Pulitzer Prize in 1956 for writing a collection of essays called *Profiles in Courage*. The book studied the lives of politicians who acted according to their principles. It was later revealed that Kennedy had perhaps bent the truth in claiming to be the sole author of the book. Apparently, the book was largely written by his staff, prompting one critic to comment that perhaps Kennedy had shown "too much profile and not enough courage."

A Rising Political Star

In 1960, Kennedy was one of the most popular Democrats in the country. He invited Lyndon Johnson to be his vice presidential running mate and together they won their party's nomination. The Republicans nominated the nation's vice president, Richard M. Nixon, to run against Kennedy.

Kennedy understood the power of the media and he frequently repeated his campaign message "We Can Do Better" to reporters. Although television was still in its infancy during his campaign, Kennedy used it to his advantage. The 1960 presidential debates were the first to be televised. On-screen, Kennedy appeared vibrant, handsome, and alert, while Nixon looked unshaven and nervous. Some 70 million Americans tuned in to watch.

The 1960 presidential election was a very close race. Election results were not known until 5:45 AM, hours after the last polling place had closed. Kennedy won by the slimmest of margins. His inaugural speech included one of the most famous lines in American history: "And so, my fellow Americans, ask not what your country can do for you; ask what you can do for your country." These words were meant to inspire the younger generation to become involved in and to trust the government. Further reflecting the sense of vitality and enthusiasm associated with his administration, Kennedy's cabinet aides and advisers came to be known as the Best and the Brightest.

Senator John F. Kennedy takes notes as then–Vice President Richard Nixon speaks during their presidential debate on September 26, 1960.

Timeline
John Fitzgerald Kennedy

May 29, 1917
John F. Kennedy is born in Brookline, Massachusetts.

1936
Kennedy enrolls at Harvard University.

1941
Kennedy joins the U.S. Navy.

1943
As a lieutenant, Kennedy takes command of a torpedo boat during World War II.

1952
Kennedy announces his candidacy for the Senate.

1953
Kennedy weds Jacqueline Lee Bouvier in Newport, Rhode Island.

1957
Kennedy's *Profiles in Courage* wins the Pulitzer Prize. Caroline Bouvier Kennedy is born.

1960
Kennedy becomes the first Catholic to be elected president. John F. Kennedy Jr. is born.

1963
President Kennedy is assassinated in Dallas, Texas.

The Presidency

When Kennedy took office the economy was booming. Many people who came of age during World War II had settled into comfortable houses in the rapidly developing suburbs and had begun raising the next generation, who would come to be known as baby boomers. Some 177 million people strong, the nation entertained itself by going to see films like Alfred Hitchcock's *Psycho* and *The Alamo* starring John Wayne. On radio and television, Frank Sinatra crooned and Elvis Presley shook his hips.

In his inauguration speech, President Kennedy urged, "...ask not what your country can do for you; ask what you can do for your country."

But there was also a great deal of national anxiety. The United States had entered into the atomic age and this caused a great deal of unease among Americans. Many feared a nuclear war. Kennedy also entered office at a time when many feared communist powers, especially the Union of Soviet Socialist Republics, or U.S.S.R. (also known as the Soviet Union), led by Premier Nikita Krushchev.

The Cold War

"Cold War" was a term used to describe the simmering tensions between the Soviet Union and the United States. The antagonism was so strong that during his presidency (1952–1960), Dwight Eisenhower ordered the construction of bomb shelters across America. Eisenhower feared that Soviet premier Nikita Krushchev would unleash a nuclear attack.

A family settles into a deluxe fallout shelter on display at Civil Defense headquarters in New York City on November 2, 1960. During the Cold War era, people thought shelters like this would protect them from nuclear war.

The cold war was often seen as a struggle between two powerful nations, or superpowers. In the United States, many politicians also described it as a competition between two forms of government: Communism and democracy. However, some have pointed out that this description is not entirely accurate: The Soviet Union was not a true communist state, nor was the United States a purely democratic one. Nevertheless, the war of words, or propaganda, that fueled the cold war pitted the Soviet Union against the United States.

During his election campaign, Kennedy promised that America could and would withstand any communist threats. This goal became a major focus of the Kennedy administration and led to the United States' involvement in Cuba and Vietnam.

Cuba

America had long been involved in the politics of Cuba, an island nation only ninety miles from the shores of the United States. The Monroe Doctrine of 1823 had been introduced to ensure that European countries did not try to colonize the United States' Latin American neighbors. The doctrine stated that the United States would consider any invasion of those countries an affront.

In return, the United States took further interest in protecting and becoming involved with those Latin American countries. In 1959, shortly before Kennedy took office, Communist rebel Fidel Castro and his supporters wrested power from the American-supported dictator Fulgencio Batista. Castro reclaimed formerly American-owned plantations in Cuba and ejected resort and gambling casino profiteers. Castro also turned to the U.S.S.R. for support.

The Bay of Pigs Invasion

This turn of events in Cuba disturbed President Kennedy. When Kennedy took office, he inherited a plan to thwart Castro that President Dwight

D. Eisenhower had devised during his presidency. Led by CIA agents, Cuban refugees trained by the U.S. military would invade the island and convince village residents to revolt en masse against the Castro government.

At first, Kennedy was reluctant to see the plan through, but eventually he gave the go-ahead for the invasion. On April 17, 1961, several American planes bombed Castro's airfields. Next, 1,500 anti-Castro Cuban exiles landed in Cuba. Kennedy refused to approve a planned second air strike fearing the loss of American lives.

MISSILE EQUIPMENT
MARIEL PORT FACILITY
4 NOVEMBER 1962

This aerial photo of missile launch sites at the Mariel Port Facility in Cuba was taken during the Cuban Missile Crisis.

Castro's forces overpowered and arrested the invading exiles. There were no mass uprisings against the government in the villages. In fact, the mission was a complete failure. Cuban American groups were none too happy with Kennedy, and although he accepted full responsibility for the disaster, he felt that he had been misled by the CIA.

The Cuban Missile Crisis

In October 1962, Kennedy faced another crisis involving Cuba. American intelligence sources had discovered that the Soviet Union was building nuclear missile sites on the Cuban coast only ninety miles from the southern tip of Florida. Kennedy demanded that the missiles be removed. The Soviets refused.

The president set up a naval blockade to inspect all ships approaching Cuba. Those that carried weapons were turned back. The U.S.S.R. defied the blockade by sending a ship through.

The tense military standoff between the two superpowers lasted for thirteen days. Finally, Krushchev promised to remove the missile sites as long as the United States agreed not to attempt any more invasions of Cuba. Kennedy agreed. The threat of immediate nuclear war was avoided. Although this garnered Kennedy a great deal of public approval, hard-line conservatives felt he had been too soft.

Vietnam

A country located in Southeast Asia, Vietnam was once a colony of France. It was divided into North and South in 1954. Ho Chi Minh was a Communist leader who had led the fight for independence from the French. He controlled North Vietnam.

During Eisenhower's term as president, America had committed itself to helping South Vietnam hold off North Vietnamese forces. President Eisenhower had also helped to install a pro-Western leader named Ngo Dinh Diem (who had supported the French) to govern South Vietnam. When Kennedy took office, military advisers were already in South Vietnam hoping to keep Ho Chi Minh's forces at bay. Although the U.S. government never declared war on North Vietnam, the number of military personnel sent to South Vietnam during the Kennedy administration rose from 5,000 to 17,000.

The War at Home

On the home front, African Americans demanded both an end to segregation and protection of their civil rights. The Reverend Dr. Martin Luther King Jr. led this nonviolent movement for social change. Police responses to restaurant sit-ins and protests, especially in Alabama, resulted in violence.

Kennedy had been reluctant to introduce civil rights legislation to Congress. This hesitancy may have stemmed from his fear of angering white southern voters and thereby endangering his chance to win a second term as president in the upcoming election. Television footage of the protests against segregation helped change his mind. Broadcast news showing police turning firehoses and police dogs on

Three demonstrators protesting segregation join hands to brace themselves against the force of water sprayed from firehoses by police during protests in Birmingham, Alabama, in 1963.

the men, women, and children of Birmingham, Alabama, forced Kennedy to take action.

Kennedy created the Civil Rights Bill. Although the bill did not pass through the Senate and House of Representatives until after his death, Kennedy wrote and championed it. The bill became a hallmark of his administration. The Civil Rights Bill proved extremely unpopular with many Americans. Even though it had not yet been officially passed into law, with the creation of the bill, Kennedy's popularity dipped to its lowest point since his election.

Behind and
Beyond the Assassination

At the time of his arrest, twenty-four-year-old Lee Harvey Oswald had already lived a few lives. He had served in the U.S. Marines; he had become a Marxist and had defected to Russia; he had returned to the United States with a Russian wife and baby; he had tried to assassinate a right-wing general, Edwin Walke; he had moved to New Orleans, Louisiana, and become involved in a pro-Castro organization; he had attempted to go to Cuba; he had killed a Dallas police officer; and, it seemed, he had assassinated the president.

By 1963, Oswald had at least two other names, or aliases, and as many guns. On the day of President Kennedy's assassination, one of those guns was found on the sixth floor of the Texas School Book Depository. Oswald had worked there for a little more than a month at the time of the shooting.

Although a good deal of evidence points to Oswald as the man who murdered Kennedy, theories abound as to who else might have been involved. Did Oswald act alone or with others? Was the Mafia or possibly the federal government connected to the shooting? Tales of conspiracies continue to circulate today.

Lee Harvey Oswald holds a rifle and a newspaper in this photograph used in the investigation of the Kennedy assassination.

Any chance to find out the truth from Lee Harvey Oswald died the afternoon of Sunday, November 24, 1963. Jack Ruby shot and killed Oswald at close range as he was being transferred from the local city lock-up to the Dallas County Jail. Television cameras recorded the entire event. Oswald was rushed to Parkland Memorial Hospital, where he was rolled down the very hallways President Kennedy had traveled only two days earlier. He was pronounced dead at 1:07 PM.

Lee Harvey Oswald's Life

Oswald's road to this unhappy end began on October 18, 1939, in New Orleans, Louisiana, when Lee was born to Marguerite Oswald. Oswald's father had died two months earlier. Many accounts describe Marguerite as a domineering woman, reportedly bitter at finding herself raising three young sons on very little money.

Marguerite sent Lee's brother, Robert, and half-brother, John-Pic, to an orphanage, Bethlehem Children's Home, and she kept Lee home with her. As a baby Lee was often shuffled among relatives. When he turned three, he joined his brothers in the orphanage.

After Marguerite remarried, she gathered up her boys and moved the family to Fort Worth, Texas. By the time he was fifteen years old, Lee Harvey Oswald and his mother had moved well over a dozen times from Louisiana to Texas to New York, and back to Louisiana again. The most recent move to New Orleans was to keep Oswald from being sent to a home for disturbed boys in New York City. There, a judge had suggested that he be removed from Marguerite's care, as she appeared unable to handle him. He rarely attended school and kept mainly to himself. He was often surly and violent with those around him.

FBI fingerprinting fluid stains Lee Harvey Oswald's military identification card. The card was found in Oswald's wallet on the day of his arrest after the assassination of President Kennedy.

At the age of seventeen, Oswald joined the marines and shipped out for Japan. Soon, he became very vocal about his interest in Marxism and Russian culture. After suffering a nervous breakdown, he was discharged from the U. S. Marine Corps, and, at the age of twenty, defected to the Soviet Union.

In the Soviet Union, he met and married Marina Prusakova. Unhappy in the Soviet Union, in the summer of 1962 Lee and Marina came back to the United States and settled in Forth Worth, Texas. Marina gave birth to a baby girl named June in February 1963. Not long after June's birth, Oswald purchased a Mannlicher-Carcano rifle using the alias A. Hidell.

Lee Harvey Oswald distributes "Hands Off Cuba" flyers on the streets of New Orleans, Louisiana, around 1962. This photograph was used as evidence against Oswald in the investigation of the assassination of President Kennedy.

In the summer of 1963, Oswald moved to New Orleans and opened a chapter of the organization Free Play For Cuba, a pro-Castro group. His admiration for Fidel Castro and Cuba increased, and he began to make plans to travel there. Since Castro had come to power, travel from the United States to Cuba was prohibited by law. Oswald attempted to enter Cuba by way of Mexico in September 1963 using his Russian residency and work papers. When his visa was rejected by the Cuban Consulate in Mexico City, he moved to Dallas, Texas, where a pregnant Marina and baby June had relocated.

The Texas School Book Depository

A friend suggested that Oswald apply for a job at the Texas School Book Depository. He did and was hired. He was assigned to the main building on Elm Street facing Dealey Plaza. His first day on the job was October 16, 1963. On October 21, Marina and Lee Harvey's second daughter, Audrey Marina Rachel, was born.

On Friday, November 22, Oswald got a ride to the depository with his coworker Buell Frazier. Frazier noticed that Oswald was carrying a long, paper package. When Frazier asked what was in it, Oswald told him curtain rods. When they arrived at work, Lee went to his space on the seventh floor. A new plywood floor was being installed on the sixth level of the depository building that day, so it was empty.

After the assassination, many eyewitnesses recalled seeing someone or something in the sixth-floor window of the book depository moments before and after President Kennedy and Governor Connally were shot. Other witnesses came forward with descriptions of a man fitting Oswald's profile boarding both a bus and a taxi heading away from the center of town immediately following the assassination. When a man fitting Oswald's description shot Officer Tippit only a few miles from the scene of the assassination, the police sprang into action.

The Aftershock

Once police caught Oswald at the Texas Theater for shooting officer J. D. Tippit, events began to unfold quickly. Dallas police began to investigate Oswald's connection to the Kennedy shooting. In 1963, the law did not guarantee a defendant's access to legal counsel at the time of arrest. Thus, at his arraignment (before the slain president's autopsy had even begun), Oswald had no lawyer. He had asked for the services of John Abt, an American Civil Liberties Union lawyer in New York, but Abt turned him down.

This photo of Lee Harvey Oswald was taken shortly after his arrest.

People both inside and outside of court began to view Oswald as a shady character. At the time of his arrest, he was carrying identification bearing two different names. On television, he appeared sullen and angry. He was also a self-professed Communist. He seemed to fit many people's idea of an assassin. Only two days after his arrest, as authorities transferred him to the

Miranda v. Arizona, 1966

When Lee Harvey Oswald was arrested in 1963, there were no Miranda Rights for a person being taken into police custody. Any comments he made could be used against him during his trial. He was also not immediately assigned a lawyer to inform him of his rights and to protect his interests. The Supreme Court's *Miranda* decision stemmed from an appeal by Ernesto Miranda, who had been convicted of kidnapping and rape in an Arizona court. During the police investigation, Miranda had confessed and then signed a written statement of his guilt without first being told that he had the right to have a lawyer present. A lawyer might have advised him to remain silent. Miranda's confession was later used at his trial to obtain his conviction.

The Supreme Court held in *Miranda v. Arizona* that the prosecution could not use his statements unless the police had made sure that his Fifth Amendment right not to implicate himself in a crime had been protected during the investigation. The *Miranda* ruling shocked the law-enforcement community and was hotly debated. Critics of the *Miranda* decision said that the Supreme Court had seriously weakened law-enforcement agencies. In later cases, the Court added limits to what are commonly referred to as a person's Miranda rights.

Nightclub owner Jack Ruby shoots Lee Harvey Oswald as the assassin is led to the county jail.

county jail, Jack Ruby approached Oswald and shot a bullet into his stomach, killing him.

A Sad End

At his funeral in Fort Worth, Texas, on Monday November 25, Oswald's mourners consisted of three adults—his widow, his mother, and his brother—two children, and a small band of journalists. In the end, these reporters carried his body to its final resting place; there was no one else there to do it. That same day, President Kennedy was being buried in Washington, D.C., attended by world leaders and a weeping public.

Public and Private Reactions

As people around the world mourned, *Air Force One* touched down at Andrews Air Force Base at 6:00 PM Friday night, bringing the slain president's body back to Washington, D.C. Robert Kennedy, the president's brother, met Jackie at the plane as JFK's aides brushed aside the soldiers waiting to remove the coffin. The aides themselves then lifted JFK's coffin off the plane and down the stairs. It had been Jackie Kennedy's idea for the aides to take hold of the coffin. She told them, "I want his friends to carry him down." They placed the coffin on the transport for Bethesda Hospital, where doctors would perform an autopsy.

During the flight Jackie had sat at the rear of the plane next to the casket. She still wore the suit she'd had on since that morning. It was covered with her husband's blood, but she refused to change it. She wanted the world to see what had been done.

Sunlight streams through the columns of the rotunda of the U.S. Capitol onto the coffin of President John F. Kennedy on November 24, 1963. The president's body lay in state in the rotunda until funeral services the next day.

The Final Weekend

Both official public and private services were scheduled for the weekend following the assassination. Monday, November 25, the day of the funeral, was declared a national holiday. It was also little John-John's third birthday.

On Sunday, November 24, a procession took Kennedy's casket to the Capitol Building, where it was laid on the same catafalque (an ornamental structure for viewing) that had held President Lincoln's coffin. People had begun to draw parallels between the death of Lincoln in 1865 and the death of Kennedy. They had both been elected to the presidency in a year ending in "60." They were both strong proponents of civil rights, cut down in their prime seemingly by political dissenters.

Television cameras filmed the ceremony. Speeches were made and flowers were lain. Jackie and young Caroline both knelt beside JFK's flag-draped coffin and the photo of that moment was seared into the public consciousness. When the ceremonies ended, the doors opened to the public.

The public's reaction was overwhelming. Kennedy's body lay in state until Monday morning. An estimated 250,000 people walked by to view it. The line outside the Capitol stretched for three miles. Television cameras stationed in the rotunda of the U.S. Capitol Building showed the faces of mourners as they walked past JFK's coffin.

The Final Journey

On Monday, the coffin was carried on a horse-drawn caisson to St. Matthew's Cathedral for a requiem mass attended by heads of state from all over the world. Millions of people lined the streets to catch a glimpse of the procession as it passed. News reports noted that instead of riding in a limousine, Jackie Kennedy had decided to walk behind the coffin from the White House to the church, eight blocks away.

When the visiting dignitaries attending the funeral learned of her plan, they insisted on walking also, throwing security agents into a panic. Not one of the dignitaries could be talked out of walking with the widow. After the mass, Kennedy's body was taken to Arlington National Cemetery, where an eternal flame was lit. That night, the family returned to the White House and held John-John's birthday party.

The World Mourns

From that deadly Friday afternoon to the funeral on Monday, the public was glued to their television sets. There were no commercials, no sports reports, and few accounts of anything other than events related to the assassination.

More than two-thirds of Americans reported experiencing symptoms ranging from nausea to headaches to depression, and many endured bouts of crying that weekend. The outpouring of grief abroad was also immense. Britain's parliament conducted a tribute to the slain American president and then adjourned. This honor was normally reserved for a British monarch or prime minister. Even Nikita Krushchev went to the American embassy in Moscow on Saturday and signed the mourning register.

The assassination of President Kennedy made headlines throughout the world.

Jack Ruby

Fifty-three-year-old nightclub owner Jack Rubenstein, also known as Jack Ruby, responded to the assassination by shooting Lee Harvey Oswald. This served only to heighten the chaos and confusion surrounding the assassination of President Kennedy. All manner of speculation swirled around Jack Ruby, but he claimed that he had killed Lee Harvey Oswald to spare Mrs. Kennedy and her children the ordeal of a trial. Ruby claimed that it was his patriotic duty to kill the President's assailant.

Ruby also explained that when he had seen what appeared to be a sneer come across Oswald's face during his televised arrest, he snapped. That's when he decided to go forward with his plan. A number of Ruby's friends claimed that the shooting was not too terribly out of character. They knew Ruby to be impulsive, starved for attention, and capable of committing such a crime.

Ruby and the Warren Commission

President Johnson formed the Warren Commission a week after Kennedy's death. They were responsible for investigating the assassination. Eight men sat on the commission (headed by the Chief Justice of the Supreme Court, Earl Warren).

Although Ruby told the Warren Commission that he had acted alone, his connections to the Mafia, also known as the Mob, were quite unsettling. Some believed that Ruby had been hired to silence Oswald for fear that he would leak evidence that would point to Mob or government involvement in the assassination. The Warren Commission investigated the alleged connections between Ruby and the Mob. They found none. But a committee in the House of Representatives was conducting an ongoing investigation into Mafia affairs. They found several links.

According to the committee, Ruby had ties to associates of Mafia chieftains Carlos Marcello and Santos Trafficante. The House also asserted that Ruby had been keeping track of Oswald's whereabouts before he shot him. The committee also compared the killing to a mob shooting or "hit."

The fact that the transfer of Oswald from the city to the county jail was running nearly an hour behind schedule also supported a number of theories regarding Ruby's motives. One theory suggests that the police, in on the shooting, waited for Ruby to appear before they moved Oswald. Another theory holds that the delay in the transfer made it impossible for Ruby to have known when Oswald would appear, and that therefore, the shooting was an act of passion.

The Trial

Jack Ruby's trial for the murder of Lee Harvey Oswald began in March 1964. His lawyer, Melvin Belli, was a flamboyant San Francisco attorney. Belli claimed that the Rubenstein family had a history of mental illness, and that Ruby was insane when he shot Oswald. The jury deliberated for less than an hour and came back with a guilty verdict. Ruby was sentenced to death.

While serving time in the Dallas County Jail at Dealey Plaza, Ruby contracted pneumonia. Doctors then discovered he had cancer of the lymph nodes. Belli had won an appeal, but while he was awaiting a new trial, Ruby died of cancer on January 3, 1967.

The Aftermath

The assassination of President Kennedy sent a
ripple effect of fear, sadness, and regret across
the nation. The American public wanted
answers. How and why had such an event happened?

The Warren Commission

The eight men, including future president Gerald
Ford, assigned to determine who had killed JFK hired
attorneys and set about investigating the crime. They
called upon the FBI, the CIA, and the Secret Service to
gather information. *Life* and the *New York Times* also
began their own probes.

In September 1964, President Johnson received an
888 page report from the Commission. Twenty-six vol-
umes containing testimony from more than 550 individ-
uals followed one month later. A condensed one-volume
Warren Report was also released to the public.

According to the report, the Mannlicher-Carcano
rifle found on the sixth floor of the depository
contained one live shell and three empty cartridge
cases. Bullet fragments removed from the limousine
and the victims came from those empty cases.

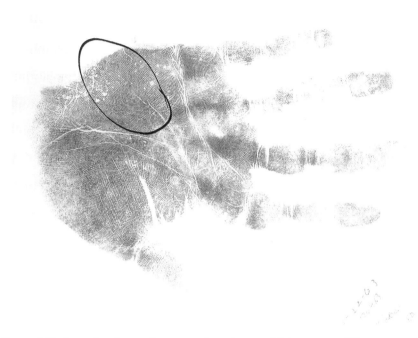

This is Oswald's handprint, taken at the time of his arrest. The area circled in red was compared to a partial palm print found on a box in the Texas School Book Depository. The prints matched.

Blanket fibers from the rifle matched those of a blanket found in the garage of Oswald's residence. Marina Oswald testified that her husband kept his rifle in that blanket. The commission concluded that Lee Harvey Oswald had acted alone in firing three successive shots in six to eight seconds. One shot missed. One bullet hit President Kennedy and caused the neck wound before it traveled out of his body and injured Governor Connally. This came to be known as the single bullet theory because it seemed incredible that one single bullet could do this much damage to both Governor Connally and President Kennedy. The third bullet did the most damage when it hit President Kennedy in the head.

Excerpts from the Warren Report

The shots that killed President Kennedy and wounded Governor Connally were fired from the sixth-floor window at the southeast corner of the Texas School Book Depository. This determination is based upon the following:

✪ Witnesses at the scene saw a rifle being fired from the sixth-floor window of the depository building, and some saw a rifle in the window immediately after the shots were fired.

✪ The nearly whole bullet found on Governor Connally's stretcher at Parkland Memorial Hospital and the two bullet fragments found in the front seat of the presidential limousine were fired from the 6.5 mm Mannlicher-Carcano rifle found on the sixth floor of the depository building to the exclusion of all other weapons.

✪ The three used cartridge cases found near the window on the sixth floor at the southeast corner of the building were fired from the same rifle that fired the above-described bullet and fragments, "to the exclusion of all other weapons. . . ."

The Warren Commission also relied on film footage made by Abraham Zapruder. Zapruder, a Dallas resident, had shot the entire assassination as he stood on the grassy knoll in front of the book depository. The government confiscated Zapruder's film. Oliver Stone's movie *JFK*, released in 1991, was the first time the public had a chance to view Zapruder's footage, although the government had released still photographs made from the footage prior to the movie's release. It has since been released to the public. That footage became the single most important transcript of the event, as it showed frame by frame the action and timing of the bullets.

Conspiracy Theories

Immediately following the assassination, most Americans believed that Oswald played a key role in the Kennedy assassination. Still, many had trouble believing that Oswald had acted alone, or as a lone gunman. A Gallup Poll taken only days after the shooting revealed that only 29 percent of Americans believed that Oswald had acted alone. After the Warren Commission released its report, 69 percent reported that they were convinced that Oswald alone was responsible for the assassination.

Even today, conspiracy theories abound regarding the assassination of President Kennedy. Some maintain Oswald's innocence and argue that a man who looked like Oswald actually committed the crime. Others believe that Oswald was involved, but argue that he was merely a pawn, working for either the Mob or for the government.

Many believe that the Warren Commission omitted or ignored key details during their investigation of the Kennedy assassination.

Secretly taped conversations in which Mafia leaders talked about wanting Kennedy dead would seem to support arguments that the Mob was involved. And JFK's brother Robert was attorney general during his administration. Robert Kennedy had relentlessly pursued organized crime leaders, especially in his investigations for the House Un-American Activities Committee. Some people have also speculated that the Cuban government may have been involved in the assassination. They contend that Cuban officials, angered by CIA plots to kill Fidel Castro, plotted to murder the president.

Others think that U.S. officials may have been behind the assassination. Prior to Kennedy's death, it was rumored that he might pull American troops out of Vietnam. Some military officials disagreed with the president. They felt that the United States should stay involved in the conflict between North Vietnam and South Vietnam. Further, they hoped that a South Vietnamese victory would stem the spread of Communism throughout Southeast Asia.

The Legacy

Immediately following Kennedy's death, President Johnson pushed a great deal of Kennedy's proposals through Congress. One of the most significant was the Civil Rights Bill that finally passed two months after Kennedy's death. In November 1964, *Look* magazine noted that "What Congress did not give Kennedy while he lived, it gave him as he lay dead." Nevertheless, national discontent was simmering just under the surface. It soon exploded.

Anti–Vietnam War protesters march down Pennsylvania Avenue towards a rally at the Washington Monument.

Military involvement in Vietnam escalated under Johnson. Although never officially declared a war, by 1968 it had become the longest military conflict in American history. Initially, the American public did not realize the extent of American losses in the jungles of Vietnam. Only after viewing television images of bloodied and injured soldiers fighting a seemingly losing battle did people understand the degree of American involvement.

At home, in 1965, the Los Angeles, California, neighborhood of Watts—a tinderbox of racial tension in the city—exploded in violence. There were further race riots in major cities across the nation, including Chicago in 1966. And, sadly, in 1968, civil rights leader Dr. Martin Luther King Jr. was assassinated in Memphis, Tennessee. Due to the many violent conflicts at home and abroad, many Americans felt as if the world was falling apart.

Camelot

Although at the conclusion of the 1960s the world seemed chaotic, the decade had started with a dream. To many Americans, John F. Kennedy was a symbol of that dream, embodying hope for a bright future and confidence in the present.

In a *Life* magazine article one month after her husband's death, Jackie used the phrase "Camelot" in reference to her husband's time in office. Camelot was King Arthur's court in twelfth-century Britain. It was host to the greatest and bravest warriors of the day, who searched for the Holy Grail. This description conveyed the power felt in the White House during the Kennedy administration. With that phrase, Jacqueline Kennedy touched the emotions of all people who wanted to believe that they had lived during a special period in America's history.

The Kennedy Era

January 1959
Cuba falls to Communist rebels.

November 1959
Fidel Castro takes power in Cuba.

October 1960
The first televised presidential debate occurs between Kennedy and Nixon.

November 1960
John F. Kennedy is elected president.

January 1960
John F. Kennedy is sworn in as the thirty-fifth president of the United States.

February 1961
The Peace Corps is launched.

Winter 1961
Kennedy creates the Green Berets.

April 1961
The Bay of Pigs invasion occurs.

April 1961
The U.S.S.R. launches cosmonaut Yuri Gagarin into space, making it the first nation to put a man into space.

May 1961
Alan Shepard becomes the first American in space.

Summer 1961
The Berlin Wall is erected.

February 1962
John Glenn is the first American to orbit Earth.

October 1962
The Cuban Missile Crisis occurs.

July 1962
The first Telstar satellite relays television programs between the United States and Europe.

The Assassination of John F. Kennedy

January 1963
Silent Spring by Rachel Carson kicks off the environmental movement.

February 1963
The Feminine Mystique by Betty Friedan launches the women's movement.

April 1963
The Reverend Dr. Martin Luther King Jr. begins desegregation efforts in Birmingham, Alabama.

May 1963
The race riots in Birmingham are televised.

June 1963
Kennedy introduces the Civil Rights Bill to Congress.

Summer 1963
The Nuclear Test Ban Treaty is signed.

August 1963
Dr. Martin Luther King Jr. gives his "I have a dream" speech at the Lincoln Memorial.

November 2, 1963
U.S.-backed Vietnamese president Diem is assassinated.

November 22, 1963
John Fitzgerald Kennedy is assassinated.

December 6, 1963
Life magazine article prints interview with Jackie, popularizing the term "Camelot."

January 1964
The Civil Rights Act is passed.

Glossary

Addison's disease Rare disease named after the English physician who discovered it. It affects the adrenal glands and often results in extreme weakness, weight loss, low blood pressure, and digestive problems.

Air Force One Official airplane used by the president.

American Civil Liberties Union Organization of lawyers who fight for people's civil rights.

antagonism Actively expressing opposition or hostility.

Arlington National Cemetery The cemetery where John F. Kennedy, his wife, and his extended family are buried. His burial space is attended by an eternal flame.

arraignment To be brought before a court of law to answer charges.

assailant One who violently attacks with words or with blows.

attorney general The chief law officer of a government.

autopsy Examination of a corpse to discover the cause of death.

baby boomers People born between the years 1946 to 1964, so named because so many children were born due to the country's prosperity and advances in medicine.

Bay of Pigs   1961 conflict between the United States and Cuba.

Capitol   Building in which the U.S. Congress meets in Washington, D.C.

caisson   Two-wheeled wagon with a chest for ammunition, drawn by horses.

catafalque   Wooden framework on which a body in a coffin lies in state.

CIA   Central Intelligence Agency, created by President Harry Truman in 1947. Coordinates the nation's intelligence activities by correlating, evaluating, and disseminating intelligence, which affects national security.

Communism   Formulated in the mid-1800s. A theory that advocates a society in which there is no private ownership, all property is shared with the community, and labor is organized for the common good of all members. The principle is that each person should work according to his or her ability and should receive compensation according to his or her needs.

FBI   The Federal Bureau of Investigation, the governmental organization that investigates federal crimes.

flamboyant   Marked by colorful displays in appearance or behavior.

Free Play For Cuba   Marxist organization promoting the ideals of Fidel Castro.

hallmark   Distinguishing character or feature.

inaugural speech   First official speech made by the president during his or her inauguration, the ceremony inducting him or her into office.

jaundice   Disease characterized by yellowness of skin, tissues, and body fluids.

laying in state   When a dignitary is laid out for viewing in his or her coffin.

Mafia   Secret society engaged in illegal activities. Also called La Cosa Nostra and the Mob.

Mannlicher-Carcano rifle   German rifle that has more precision due to its long barrel.

Marxism   A form of socialism in which all things in society are shared. Formed by Karl Marx and Friedrich Engels in the mid-1800s, Marxist thought is based on a society where production, distribution, and exchange is equal among all people. Close in thought to Communism, generally opposed to capitalism.

Monroe Doctrine of 1853   Enacted by the United States to protect Latin American countries from European domination.

Parliament   Official government council of England.

Pulitzer Prize   Established by Joseph Pulitzer in 1911. An annual prize for literary and/or journalistic achievement.

rotunda   Round building, hall, or room, often with a dome.

Secret Service   Branch of the treasury used to protect the president, the president's family, and aides.

Senate   Upper house of the Congress or of most of the state legislatures.

sit-ins   Forms of protest whereby people literally sit down in a place where they are not wanted.

They usually practice passive resistance—letting themselves be dragged away—when being removed by police.

sniper Individual who shoots from a hidden position.

UPI news service United Press International news wire began in America in the early 1900s to disseminate news all over the world.

vice president Official next in rank below a president. Acts as president in the event of the president's absence or incapacity.

wrest To gain with difficulty, by force or as if by force.

For More Information

Assassination Archive and Research Center (AARC)
918 F Street NW, Room 510
Washington, DC 20004
(202) 393-1917

Committee for an Open Archives (COA)
P.O. Box 6008
Washington, DC 20005
(202) 310-1858

The Conspiracy Museum
110 South Market Street
Dallas, TX 75202
(214) 741-3040
e-mail: tcm95@altinet.net

John Fitzgerald Kennedy Library
Columbia Point
Boston, MA 02125
(877) 616-4599
Web site: http://www.cs.umb.edu/jfklibrary

John F. Kennedy National Historic Site
83 Beals Street
Brookline, MA 02446
(617) 566-1689
Web site: http://www.nps.gov/jofi

The Sixth Floor Museum at Dealey Plaza
411 Elm Street
Dallas, TX 75202-3308
(214) 747-6660
Web site: http://www.jfk.org

Web Sites

The History Place: John F. Kennedy Photo History
http://www.historyplace.com/kennedy/gallery.htm

JFK Assassination Research Materials
http://www.jfk-info.com

John F. Kennedy Biography
http://www.whitehouse.gov/history/presidents/
    jk35.html

National Archives and Records Administration
The President John F. Kennedy Assassinations
    Records Collection
http://www.nara.gov/research/jfk

For Further Reading

Callahan, Bob. *Who Shot JFK?: A Guide to the Major Conspiracy Theories*. New York: Simon & Schuster, 1993.

Groden, Robert. *The Killing of a President*. New York: Penguin Books, 1994.

Hunt, Conover. *JFK for a New Generation*. Dallas, TX: Southern Methodist University Press, 1996.

Levy, Peter B., ed. *America in the Sixties—Right, Left, and Center*. Westport, CT: Greenwood Publishing Group, 1998.

Posner, Gerald. *Case Closed: Lee Harvey Oswald and the Assassination of JFK*. New York: Anchor Books, 1994.

Selkirk, Errol. *JFK for Beginners*. 2nd ed. New York: Writers and Readers, 2001.

Index

Index

About The Author

Lauren Spencer is originally from California and now lives in New York City, where she teaches writing workshops in the public schools. She also writes lifestyle and music articles for magazines.

Photo Credits

Cover Photo and pp. 1, 14, 23 © The John F. Kennedy Library/National Archives; pp. 4, 9, 10, 11, 19, 24, 26, 29, 34, 40, 50 © Bettmann/Corbis; p. 12 © Records of the House Select Committee on Assassinations; pp. 16, 31, 33, 47 © Records of the Warren Commission; p. 21 © AP Wide World Photos; National Archives; pp. 36, 38, © Hulton/Archive; p. 43 © Carl Mydans/Timepix; p. 51 © Wally McNamee/Corbis.

Series Design and Layout

Les Kanturek